The publisher is not responsible for the views expressed herein, which are not necessarily those of the author.

p&p
publishing

How to Insult the

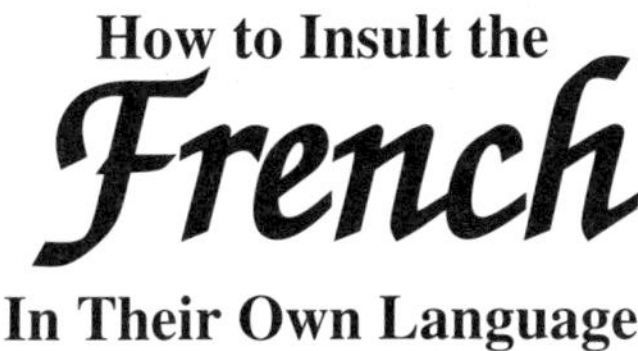

In Their Own Language

by P. W. Risdon

additional material

Patrick Vidaud

p&p publishing is an imprint of Editgrange Limited

How to Insult the French in their own Language
by P.W. Risdon

with additional material, linguistic expertise
and illustrations by Patrick Vidaud

P & P Publishing is an imprint
of Editgrange Limited
P.O. Box 13, 101 Clapham High Street,
London SW4 7TB

ISBN 1 900282 00 3

Printed by Ross Perkins, London W11 1JN

Preface

This phrase book is designed to plug a much neglected gap in the market. So many misunderstandings can arise between people who do not understand each other's language. The other person might suspect you are being abusive, but how can they really know? Now, with the aid of this little book, you can ensure they are in no doubt. And of course, when insulting someone, it is so much more polite to use their native tongue.

Part 1 covers all the grammar you're likely to need, which isn't very much, and gives an overall view of French swearwords, profanities and terms of abuse. Part 2 is designed to help with daily mundanities such as eating, sleeping and getting into fights over parking spaces. If you use this book a great deal on your trip to France, you might find it helpful to refer to Part 3. The prison authorities will probably let you keep a copy in your cell.

Part 4 covers a range of conversation topics. The French are extremely sensitive about, well, almost everything. A selection of their weakest points are covered. In contrast to some of the earlier sections, what might appear to be softer insults are in fact more likely to provoke apoplexy in your new found friends than any amount of open hostility or swearing.

For general rapid use, there is a two page Quick-Reference Guide packed full of characteristically Gallic epithets practically guaranteed* to deeply offend even the most thick-skinned of our geographically closest cousins in the big happy family that is Europe.

* That is, not guaranteed.

Finally, we have left a blank page for your own field notes.

We hope this will help you to get the most from your next trip to France, although it will, of course, come in handy should you meet any French tourists in this country, or anywhere else for that matter. Believe me, they can crop up anywhere.

Contents

Part 3 - Dealing with the French Authorities

Part 4 - Conversation Topics

Introduction

It would of course be so much more convenient if everybody in the world spoke English but, sadly, they don't. Whatever the purpose of your visit to France, be it business, pleasure or, most likely, simply trying to drive through as quickly as possible on your way to Spain, you will sometimes find you need to talk to someone who has not made the effort. A depressing thought.

Fortunately, there is some hope for the future. As you will soon discover if you ever visit those great French institutions, EuroDisney or the

Paris branch of McDonalds, efforts are being made to turn the French language into English. This is a surprisingly progressive step for our cousins across the channel to make and, despite the occasional whinge from various so-called 'intellectuals' and politicians, it has been very successful so far.

So do not be surprised if you hear a French person mention '**le shopping**' or '**le weekend**'. Just give them a quiet smile of encouragement. They need it. There has been talk in the **Assemblée Nationale** (French for 'Parliament') of making the use of an English word or phrase punishable by imprisonment or worse (have you heard any French Pop music recently?).

As things stand, however, at some point during your trip to France, you're going to need to communicate in a non-English language. Maybe you'll have bought a 'Learn French by Magic in Twenty Minutes' course of books and cassettes. You'll certainly take a handy pocket-sized phrase book.

Three weeks later, you'll be standing sweating on the forecourt of a service station near Lyons, thumbing through it while some thirty-stone local farmer with forearms like varicosed legs of mutton stands there spitting and swearing in a voice like a bull with its balls trapped in a drain cover and all you'll be able to find will be "Where is the Railway Station?" and "My suitcases are in the gazebo".

No more. With the quiet flame of self-confidence in your eyes, you can snap your copy of 'How to Insult the French...' from your bum-bag. Perhaps you might flick to the section on 'Driving'. Alternatively, 'Describing Physical Appearance' could be appropriate. Or maybe a few carefully chosen remarks from the 'Quick-Reference Insult Guide' would shut the bastard up.

If you have taken the time and trouble to master a few of the simple remarks in 'Basic Abuse and Swearing', you won't even need to open this book. A couple of well-aimed epithets and you'll be on your way. Where and how will, of course, depend on whether anything well-aimed came back from the farmer. I'm afraid some of these overseas folk are a bit unpredictable.

Part 1

Preliminary

1. Some General Points

Regrettably, it is difficult to avoid some discussion of the French language. Let's keep it to a minimum, though.

For some strange reason, they have two words for 'you'. The singular, **'tu'** (<too>), is used when you are talking to one person and the plural, **'vous'** (<voo>), is used when you are talking to more than one person. Except that it isn't polite to use **'tu'**, so you use **'vous'** when you are talking to one person, unless that person is a child, in which case you would use **'tu'**. But they would use **'vous'**. Unless, of course, the person you are talking to is a good friend or family member, in which case it isn't rude to use **'tu'**. In fact, it's polite. Friendly, even. Though it isn't friendly for someone to call you **'tu'**, unless they are being friendly. And vice versa.

Simple enough, really. For our present purposes, call people **'vous'** unless you want to be rude to them. Then you'd call them **'tu'**. So I suppose we're going to be calling people **'tu'** most of the time. Unless there are several of them, in which case it's **'vous'**.

French words have gender, which means they are either masculine or feminine. I wouldn't bother too much about this, if I were you. But, if you fancy a little variation, you could use the 'feminine' insults you'll find later on for men, and the 'masculine' ones for women. The only problem with this is that the person you are insulting might think you've just made a mistake. Anyway, try it if you like.

Guides to the pronunciation of French words

are given in funny brackets. In some ways, there is a temptation to not bother trying to pronounce the words properly. After all, no one asked them to thrust their lower lips out and clear their throats all the time. However, if you really want them to understand what you are saying, and of course the full effect of a good insult is diminished if the target can't follow it, some attempt at the correct expression must be made. For obvious reasons, wherever possible the guide to pronunciation is given by using the English word which sounds most similar, whatever it might mean.

This means the pronunciation of **'tu'** is given as <too>, which you probably noticed at the start of this chapter. The ordinary brackets are used there because the pronunciation was given in brackets, which won't always be the case, although the pointy brackets will always be used. If you're not clear about this, re-read the paragraph about **'tu'** and **'vous'**.

A key point in the pronunciation of French is liaison. This is where the end of one word is, in some circumstances, run into the beginning of the next. For example, **'vous allez'**, (you go) is not pronounced as it is written, <vooz allay>, but rather as <voo zallay>. If you're wondering what I'm blathering on about, I only bother to mention this because one of the most commonly heard expressions in France ought, in theory, to be pronounced with a liaison, but isn't.

I'm talking about **'pas encore',** which means 'not yet'. It is pronounced <pah on-core>, rather than <pa's-zon-core>. You'll hear it almost everywhere. 'Is my meal ready yet?' **'Pas encore'.** 'Are my car repairs finished yet?' **'Pas encore'.** Need I go on?

If you want to be hip, begin every sentence with **'Donc...'** <donk> and end it with **'...quoi?'** <kwa>. Thus, **'T'as la tête d'un hareng effrayé'** <Tah lah tett done arran eff-fray-yea>, 'You look like a startled herring' becomes **'Donc, t'as la tête d'un**

hareng effrayé, quoi?' This is an affectation of the young in France and is a little bit like the Edwardian English habit of saying 'What!' at the end of every sentence.

'Quoi' actually means 'what'. **'Donc'** means 'therefore', except when used in this context, when it means 'I'm trying to think what to say next'. It can be spoken very slowly, <doooooooohhhhhhh-hhnnnnnnnnnnnk> - take as much as four or five seconds over it. **'Quoi',** by contrast, is spat out in triumph at having managed to string a sentence together.

If you are going to try this style of conversation, it helps to take some drugs first.

Those readers who want to go the whole hog and actually *look* like a hip young French person should try to capture the sort of effect you'd get if a late '80s American gangsta rappa fell into an industrial blender with an extra from Saturday Night Fever.

Pronunciation

The following guide will help you with the system of transliteration used in this book.

Word	As In	Rhyme
pa	father	jar
ate	consumed	vet
tear	cry	here
eh	what?	hay
yea	yes	way
-oo		you
mwa/twa/vwa/kwa		jar
duh/juh		the (short form)

Thus :

ne t'inquete pas, or 'don't worry', becomes **<nut-tank ate pa>**

2. Basic Abuse & Swearing

Swearing

People sometimes say that swearing is a sign of a limited vocabulary. This is not true. If anything, swearing automatically and naturally in a foreign language is a sign of fluency. However, there are not that many commonly used swearwords, so if they were used throughout the phrases that come in the following chapters, it would all get a bit repetitive.

This chapter explains how to swear and

gives some of the most common abusive epithets used in spoken French today. You can use this material as, when and if you like. It isn't necessary but, on the other hand, it would add a little colour and authenticity to your language.

The two most commonly used swearwords in French are **putain** <poo-tah> and **merde** <mare-duh>. If you hit your thumb with a hammer, you can combine them and shout **putain de merde** <poo-tah duh mare-duh>.

Merde means 'shit', and is used in exactly the same way as in English, as well as for emphasis by adding **de merde** <duh mare-duh> to another expression.

Putain means 'whore', and is the equivalent of 'fucking'. Thus 'the fucking car won't start' would be **la putain de voiture ne démarre pas** <lah poo-tah duh vwah-ture nuh day-mar pa>.

Connerie <connery> is the same as 'bullshit'. Out of interest, this has led to image problems in France for Sean Connery. It is as if a French film star were called Jean-Pierre Bullshit.
Qu'est-ce que c'est cette connerie là? <Kes-kuh-say set connery lah> is 'what's that bullshit?', or even 'what the fuck's that?'
C'est de la connerie <say duh lah connery> means 'this is bullshit', or 'it's bullshit'.
Arrête tes conneries <arr-et tay connery> means 'stop fucking about', or 'cut the crap'.

Cul <coo> means 'arse'. **Trou de cul** <true duck-you> is 'arsehole'. **Mon cul** <mon coo> means 'my arse', as in **La France, mon cul.**
Coup cigare <coop-cigar> is slang for 'anus'.
Fesse <fess> is equivalent to 'bum'.

Bite <beat> and **Charles le chauve** *<sharl lush-oaf> are slang for 'penis'
Couilles <cooee-yuh> means 'balls'.
Male masturbation can be referred to as **branler**

*** Bald Charles**

<bran-lay>, **astiquer** <a-stick-eh>, **agacer le sous préfet** <aga-say luh soup-ray-fay> and **étrangler le borgne** <ate-wrangler lab born>*
Jute <jute-eh> is used for 'sperm'.

Zizi <zee-zee> and **fente** <font> mean 'vagina'.
Clito <klee-toe> is equivalent to 'clitoris'.
Lo-lo <low-low> means 'tits'.

Pourri <pooh-ree> means 'rotten'. **C'est de la merde pourri** <say duh lah mare-duh pooh-ree> is a common expression, understandably, in France, meaning 'this is rotten shit'.

Sacré <sah-kray> translates roughly as 'bloody'. 'What a bloody cretin' would be **quelle sacré crétin** <kell sah-kray kray-tah>.
Bon sang <bon song> is equivalent to 'bloody hell'.

Bon Dieu <bon d'yuh> means 'good God'. For added emphasis, **bon Dieu de merde** <bon d'yuh duh mare-duh> is often used.

* These expressions translate literally as *to polish the sub-prefect* and *to strangle the one-eyed person.*

Abuse

Vas te faire foutre <vat fair foo-truh> is the closest equivalent to 'fuck off'.

Tu me fais chier <tomb fay shay> means, literally, 'you make me shit' but it is used like 'you're pissing me off', 'you're a pain in the arse'.
Fais pas chier <fay pah shay> means 'don't make me shit', 'don't bug me'.

Suce ma bite <sooce mah beet> means 'suck my cock', and has largely replaced **fais moi une pipe** <fay mwa oon peep>, which means the same thing.

Ferme ta gueule <firm tah girl> is 'shut your mouth'
La ferme <lah firm> and **'Tais toi** <tay-twa> both mean 'shut up'.

Je m'en torche <Juh mon torsh> means 'I wipe my bottom with it' and is often used to belittle something. In practice, you can drop the '**je**' and just grunt **m'en torche** <mon torsh> if you disagree with someone.

Je te casse la gueule <jute kass lah girl> is 'I'm gonna smack you in the mouth'. Bear in mind that, when people say this kind of thing in France, with a few exceptions, such as in a waterfront bar in Marseilles, they don't mean it. If you happen to be in Marseilles and decide you want to try this, you can add **dehors, tout de suite** <door, toot sweet>, which means 'outside, now'. If you then get stabbed or shot, don't come crying to us.

Vous foutez de ma gueule? <voo foo-tay duh mah girl> means 'you taking the piss?'. **Vous me moquez?** <voo muh mock-ay> is a more polite version of this.

Ça a tout foutu en l'air <saah toot foo-too on lair> means 'that's fucked everything'.
A more concise version is **c'est foutu** <say foo-

too>, or ‘it’s/that’s fucked’.

Quelle bordel <kell bordell> is ‘what a shambles’. In polite company, substitute **bazar** <baz-zar> for **‘bordel’.**

Insults For Men

Salaud	<sallow>	bastard
Mec	<meck>	jerk*
Con	<cong>	cunt
Fils de pute	<fees duh poot>	son of a bitch
Fumier	<fooh-me-yea>	bastard
Pédé	<pay-day>	pouffe
Salope	<sallow-pa>	whore
Couillon	<coo-yong>	cretin
Crétin	<kray-tah>	cretin
Idiot	<eed-yo>	idiot
Enculé	<on-coo-lay>	one who has been buggered†
Cocu	<cock-coo>	cuckold

* on the streets, this just means ‘bloke’

† this comes from the verb ‘enculer’, meaning ‘to bugger’. Try **il passe son temps à enculer les mouches** <eel pass sawn torn ah on-coo-lay lay moosh>, 'he spends his time buggering flies'. This means someone is just buggering about.

Insults for Women

Pute	<poot>	bitch, whore
Salope	<sallow-pah>	whore
Putain	<poo-tah>	whore*
Conasse	<con-ass>	silly bitch
Cocue	<cock-you>	someone whose husband sleeps around

Feel free to vary things a little. **Sale** <zal> means 'dirty, filthy'. You can say **'sale couillon', 'couillon de merde'** and so on. It's a bit like a pick-&-mix sweet counter. For example, you might find yourself wanting to construct a phrase like **il est con, ce mec** <eel ay cong, sir meck>. You should be able to figure out the meaning of this from the vocabulary given above.

Be creative. Enjoy!

* you can probably sense a pattern emerging

Part 2

Day to Day Requirements

1. Driving

Most of the road signs you will see in France are copied from the British ones, although they still persist in using the French language with monotonous regularity. Since you can't be expected to brake suddenly and look everything up, the best thing is to ignore anything you don't immediately understand although, for legal reasons, I must advise you to ignore that last piece of advice. Incidentally, diversions are called **'déviations',** in a rare moment of honesty.

There are untold bizarre regulations and laws

governing driving, with on the spot fines if you break them, so you might want to skip this section completely and turn to the chapter on 'Dealing With Police'. Like many things in France, the traffic laws are little more than a system of secondary taxation. Even the speed limits change when it rains, and exactly how you can be expected to keep track of that is beyond me.

You have to pay tolls on most of the main motorways, which they call **'autoroutes'.** Signs saying **'péage'** indicate these routes. If you decide to avoid them and stick to the alternative roads, watch for oncoming cars flashing their headlamps. This is a warning that there are police up ahead. That, or the wheel is about to come off your car, which amounts to the same thing.

Never let your fuel tank become more than half-empty. Away from the toll roads and major cities, most Service Stations close by 10:00pm, sometimes earlier. You will find yourself driving through deserted, shuttered villages. Occasionally, you might catch a sight of an elderly yokel staring with unmasked hatred at your car.

If female, she will be wearing something like a lemon yellow dress, decorated with orange flowers, a shapeless red cardigan, old stockings falling below her knees and carpet slippers. Young men will have trousers inherited from their grandfather and a striped shirt. The older men sport hats of various descriptions, on the lower lip will be a yellow cigarette they lit in 1963, and have never seen any reason to change.

If any of them have just one eye, in the middle of their forehead, pretend not to notice. Intermarriage is common in rural France. This is the reality of the peasant society our taxes prop up by way of the Common Agricultural Policy. France has more in common with Southern Italy than Germany or Britain.

I'm not even going to attempt to explain the driving laws in the towns. You have to give way at the most unexpected moments; pointless one-way systems abound - a town with just three streets will have one-way traffic around its square. They just love signs, prohibitions and laws.

You could always forget the following phrases and hire a French car. Then adopt one of two driving styles, according to your temperament. You could crawl along at about half the speed conditions permit, cigarette in mouth and completely without expression. Or drive like a maniac, shouting incoherently, waving your arms and making offensive gestures. Either way, everyone who sees you will just assume you are French. A high price to pay, but the choice is yours.

Good luck.

I'd like to hire a Vauxhall, please.

Je voudrais louer une voiture de marque Vauxhall, s'il-vous plaît.

<Shove-who-dray loo-eh oon vwat-you're dam-arc Vauxhall, seal-voo-play>

How about a Ford then?

Donc un Ford peut-être?

<Duncan Ford put-ate-ruh>

Jesus, I don't want a Renault!
Haven't you got a Skoda?

Jesu, je ne veux pas un Renault!
Vous n'avez pas un Skoda?

<Yea-sue, John voo-pa's an Renault.
Voo navvie-pa's an Skoda>

Get outta my way!

Tire toi de là!

<Tear twa duh lah>

What is that, one of those kit cars or what?

C'est quoi, ça? Une bagnole assemblée à la maison ou quoi?

<Sake wah, sah? You'n ban-yoll ass-sawm-blay ah lah maize-on ooh kwa>

Alright, calm down. You're not setting fire to lorry loads of lamb now.

Allez, calme-toi. T'est plus là à flamber des camions d'agneaux!

<Allay, calm twa. Tape-loo lah ah flaw-bay day come-yong dan-yoh>

You're on the wrong side of the road, you prat! *

Eh, couillon, t'est sur la mauvaise coté de la route.

<Hay, coo-yong, tay sir lah more-ways coat-aid Allah root>

Come on, you bastard!

Allez, salaud!

<Allay, sallow>

* Careful with this one.

2. Hotels

The nightmare scenario. You actually have to spend at least one night in France. Maybe it can't be avoided, so you'll have to make the best of it.

Smaller hotels are called **'Logis'** (<Loh-she>) or **'Auberges'** (<Oh-bear-jah>). Some of them, especially in the south, hang up signs saying **'Pension'** (<Paw-see-aw>). Owners tend to be elderly with a great deal of facial hair. Their husbands rarely get involved in the business.

The desk is normally occupied by a teenage niece or grand-daughter who cannot find any of the room keys and spends all her time chatting to a sallow youth with a moped parked outside. She will only understand English if money is being discussed.

You will find most French hotels are fairly cheap. If you are trying to find one on spec, you will also notice they are rare and either closed or fully booked. In the countryside, there are occasional signs for **'gîtes'** (<sheet>), a sort of self-catering farmhouse establishment, but these signs point down narrow empty lanes and are erected, I imagine, as an elaborate practical joke. Stick to the larger towns.

Signs saying **'Formule'** do not indicate motor racing tracks, but a chain of hotels. It's a stupid name, but they like it. **Formule** hotels are one of France's success stories, which should be warning enough. They are all very similar, rather like branches of McDonalds, except that they do not sell hamburgers. Or Chicken McNuggets. So perhaps there is something to be said for them after all.

Luxury hotels are called **'Relais'** (<Ruh-

lay>) or **'Châteaux'** (<Shat-toe>). One thing to watch out for - the Town Hall is called the **'Hôtel de Ville'.** I'm afraid this is the sort of thing you are going to have to put up with if you visit France. If you want the town hotel, you need to say **'Hôtel de *la* Ville'. 'La'** means 'the'. It is known as a direct article and makes a big difference to Johnny Foreigner.

But enough grammar. Here are some helpful phrases for booking into hotels. If you want to book into the Town Hall, you're on your own.

Excuse me, I seem to have been given keys to the airing cupboard by mistake.

Excusez-moi, il me semble que vous m'avez donné par erreur les clefs du chauffe linge.

<Ex-ewes-say-mwa, eel mass saw-bell ka voo mav-eh dough-nay par air-err lay clay dew show-phalange>

The bed is too soft, hard, long, short, small.

Le lit est trop doux, dûr, long, cort, petit.

<Lull lea ate row do, do'er, long, cor, petty>

The view is too flat, hilly, open, wooded, dark, light.

La vue est trop plate, montagneuse, ouverte, boisée, sombre, claire.

<Love-you ate row plate, mont-an-you-sah, ooh-vairt, bwa-say, som-bruh, clare>

Can you watch British T.V. here?

Peut-on regarder les émissions Britaniques ici?

<Put-on regard-ale-lay seam-is-yon britain-eek E.C.>

I prefer Irish linen.

Je préfère le linge irlandais.

<Juh prof-earl lull-lawn-jeer-lawn-day>

Nice wallpaper.

Joli papier peint.

<Show-leap pap-pea-ape-pant>

And what would a room for my pig cost?

Et combien coute-elle une chambre pour mon cochon?

<Ache om-bee-an coot-ell oon charm-bruh pour monk-coach-on>

What's this?

C'est quoi ça?

<Sake-wah sah>

You're joking!

Vous plaisantez!

<Voo plays-aunt-tay>

You taking the piss? That room hasn't been cleaned since the War.

Vous foutez de ma gueule? Cette chambre n'a pas été nettoyé depuis la guerre.

<Voo foot-aide-mag-girl? Set charm-Brunner-pa's-ate-a-net-why-aid-up-wee lag-air>

This is the filthiest, most unpleasant hotel I have ever seen.

Cet hôtel est le plus degueuelasse et désagréable que j'ai jamais connue.

<Set oh-tell ay lap-loo day-girl-lass aide days-are-grey-ab kuh jay jam-make con-ooh>

Just a bidet and a wash basin? Where I come from, we wash our whole body.

Cuvette et bidet seulement? Chez-nous, on se lave le corps entier.

<Coo-vet eh bee-day sir-lamont? Shane-nuance sir lav luck core on-tea-yeah>

This bill is extortionate. I'm not paying.

Cette note est exorbitante. Je ne paye pas.

<Set not eh ex-or-beet aunt. John pay pa>

3. Restaurant Etiquette

The gulf between the French attitude to food and that of the English speaking world is not as great as it used to be. However, despite the fact that you can read articles giving ten perfect recipes for stuffed fennel in every issue of every colour supplement published with your Sunday newspapers, there are still some differences.

The Gallic habit of torturing your food before you kill it has not quite caught on yet, for example. *We* don't keep calves in veal crates, never letting their big limpid brown eyes catch a sight of the dewy, sun-lit pastures that are their birthright. No, we picket ports in a desperate attempt to save the moist-nosed little blighters from such a fate, then import our veal from Holland and Belgium. Not from France. We have our principles and we are sticking to them.

But even though the British middle-classes now serve their roast rack of lamb pink and moist, pricked with garlic and garnished with a rosemary twig, it is still statistically more common to roast your half-shoulder for five hours, until it can be crumbled rather than carved, and to begin cooking the vegetables before the meat so that each mouthful can be effortlessly forced into your cheeks through the gaps between your teeth.

The type of insult you might choose will, therefore, depend on your attitude to food. Service in France is notoriously bad, so even if you like their food you can focus on this. Cruelty is a stalwart fallback. If, on the other hand, the only spice you use in your cooking is salt, you'll hate the food and be able to attack every aspect of it with relish.

No thanks. I don't eat veal, for ethical reasons.

Non, merci. Je ne mange pas du veau, pour des raisons morales.

<Gnaw, mercy. John mournge pa'd you've oh, pour lay rays-on more-al>

And is the lamb British or New Zealand?

Et l'agneau, il vien de Grande-Bretagne ou de Nouvelle Zélande?

<Ay lawn-yoh, eel vee-end dug raw Brit-an-yah oo noo-well zay-lawned>

Do you sell anything that hasn't been tortured?

Vendez-vous rien qui n'a pas été torturé?

<Vaughn-dave voo ree-an key nap-pa's ate-eh tort-two-ray>

I ordered twenty minutes ago. What's the chef doing? Trying to catch the cow?

J'ai commandé il y a vingt minutes. Le chef, qu'est-ce

qu'il fait? Essaie-t-il d'attraper la vache, où quoi?

Jay com-monday il-ee-ah van me-newt. Lush sheff, kess-keel-fay? Essay- tilda-trap-eh love-ash, oo kwa>

And what's that made of?

Et ça, c'est fabriqué de quoi?

<Eh-sah, say fab-ree-kay duh kwa>

You certainly use every part of the animal.

Vous essayez assurément d'utiliser tout l'animaux.

<Voos essay-eh assure-eh-mon duty-lee-say toot lan-ee-mow>

Wouldn't it be kinder to bury it?

Serait-il pas plus gentil de l'enterrer?

<Sir-ate ill pa-plew shun-till duh lawn-tare-eh>

That looks lovely. Could you ask the chef to cook it now, please.

C'est joli, ça. Pourriez-vous demander au chef de le cuire maintenant, s'il vous plaît.

<Say jolly, sah. Pour-re-ay voo duh-monday oh sheff duh luh queer man-ton-naunt, sill voo play>

Could I have a towel and a bucket, please.

Une serviette et un seau, s'il vous plaît.

<Oon serve-viet eh ah-so, sill voo play>

I'd like a bottle of Australian Chardonnay, please.

Je veux une bouteille de Chardonnay Australien, s'il-vous plaît.

<Shove-a you'n boot-tail duh shard-don-eh ost-rally-ann, sill voo play>

And a bottle of Buxton Spring Water.

Et une bouteille d'eau minérale de Buxton s'il-vous plaît.

<Eh-un boot-tail doe mean-eh-rull duh Buxton, sill voo play>

I prefer pumpernickel.

Je préfère du pumpernickel.

<Jup-ref-air do pump-err-nickel>

Cognac? No, I'll have a Scotch.

Un cognac? Non, je prends un scotch.

<An con-yak? Gnaw, juh prawn an scotch>

Put this in a bag, please. I'll see if my dog will eat it.

Mettez-le dans un sac, s'il-vous plaît. Je vais voir si mon chien le mangerait.

<Met-ale-luh dawns an sack, sill voo play. Shove-eh vwa sea maw shee-an lemon-jer-ray>

Service not included? You're right.

Service non compris? Non, vous avez raison.

<Serve-eece non com-pree? Gnaw, voo savvy rays-on>

4. Bars & Cafés

Cafés are often so small there isn't room to swing a cat, even if you've brought one specially. Best to sit outside then, particularly if the place has a **'terasse'.** Surprisingly enough, this is French for 'terrace', which is the place they put the tables and chairs, even if it looks like the pavement to your untutored eye.

It is very French to drink **'anis',** also known as **'pastis',** on the terasse. Ricard is the most common brand name. Pernod is not far behind. If you haven't tried Pernod and blackcurrant in your favourite disco at home, you haven't lived. It is second only to Malibu and pineapple juice for recreating the exotic tastes of far away places. What's more, it often vividly recreates its own taste several hours after being drunk.

The café terasse is a meeting place and a vantage point from which to watch the world, and a lot of French people, go by. Thus, you will find some other chapters useful here. 'Describing Physical Appearance', for example. 'Restaurant Etiquette' will be useful if you decide to eat anything.

If you are a smoker, you might actually quite like the French attitude. It is perfectly acceptable to smoke whilst other people are eating, between courses, between mouthfuls, even between chews. Compulsory non-smoking areas are indicated by the signs on the walls, showing you cannot smoke. You might not notice them at first, because they tend to be full of people smoking.

There is normally just the one toilet, used by both men and women, often at the same time. Do not be unnerved if, whilst you are shedding some of the evening's refreshments, the chef sticks his head through a hole in the wall and asks you how you want your steak cooked. It is a very practical arrangement.

Beyond the larger cities, when strangers enter a café all the conversations stop immediately and everyone looks at the newcomers with hostility and suspicion. Do not worry about this, it's all part of the Gallic tradition of hospitality. Just sit at a table and wait to be served. When you get tired of waiting, go to the bar and ask for whatever it is you want. If they still ignore you, go round and help yourself. You will then command their attention, if only because you owe them money.

In very small villages, bars tend to offer little food and a tiny range of drink. Anyone inside them will either be the owners or their cousins. It is bad form to swat any of the flies which swarm inside these places. They are company for the proprietors during the weeks that pass between customers; many of them answer to their names and, like small dogs, can perform a few amusing tricks.

Can we have some service here!

Du service. Ici!

<Deuce service. E.C.>

A bottle of Grolsch for my friend.

Une bouteille de Grolsch pour mon ami(e).

<Oon boot-tail dug Grolsch pour mon am-ee>

And I'll have a Stella.

Et une Stella pour moi.

<A tune Stella pour mwa>

Do you always serve beer in egg-cups?

Vous servez toujours la bière dans des coquetiers?

<Voo survey too-sure lah bee-air dawn day cock-at-chairs>

This is rotten shit. Take it back to the pisser.

C'est de la merde pourri. Renvoyez-moi ça au pissoire.

<Say duh lah mare-duh poo-ree. Ron-vwa-yea mwa sah oh piss-wah>

Where do I go for a piss?

Où est-ce qu'on mouille ses godasses*?

<Oo esk-on mousse say god-ass>

Excuse me, is this the kitchen or the toilet?

Excusez-moi, c'est le toilet ou la cuisine ici?

<Ex-ewes-say-mwa, say luh twa-let ooh lah queee-seen E.C.>

Can you tell me, is there a nice café near here?

Dites-moi. Y'a-t-il un café bien près d'ici?

<Deet-mwa. Yat-eel uh caff-ay be-yan pray D.C.>

For God's sake clean this table.

Nettoyez cette table, Bon Dieu.

***to moisten one's shoes**

<Net-twa-yea set tar-blur, bon d'yuh>

Forget it. Just bring me the bill.

Oubliez-moi ça. La note, s'il vous plaît.

<Ooh-blee-eh-mwa sah. Lah note, seal voo play>

5. Fashion & Shopping

France is, as anyone who happens to be French will tell you, the international centre for world fashion. The French therefore pride themselves on their sense of elegance and style. Let's examine this for a moment.

Every year there is a round of fashion shows in Paris. Designers show off their new **'couture'** repertoire. They vie with each other to produce the most revolutionary, radical and inspired collection of the season. Lights dim, music swells and some of the most expensive models in the world, women who don't get out of bed for less than £10,000, sashay down the catwalk wearing tin foil waistcoats, leopard skin knee-warmers and almost nothing else.

In the audience brains dim, egos swell and women who don't get into bed for less than £10,000 vie with millionairesses, editors of fashion magazines and chain-store buyers to see who can produce the most radical and inspired bankers draft of the year.

But it's not exactly street clothing, is it? You don't see many people popping out for some bread sticks and a bag of cat litter in a satin and rice-paper body sleeve inspired by the processional garb of eighteenth-century Andalusian monks. Obviously, nobody wears these clothes. So what do the French walk about in?

Those who can afford them wear British clothes. The former Prime Minister, Edouard Balladur, was famous for his well-tailored English suits, whilst wealthy businessmen are most at home in Scottish tweeds. Those who cannot afford these luxuries are forced to fall back on French equivalents. But we should have a little compassion for them. They do not buy French products because they want to. Cruel economic necessity forces them into this humiliating position.

People in the larger towns are often, at first glance, just like their equivalents in any major world city. Nowadays, fashions in Stuttgart are little different to those in Bristol, Anchorage, Adelaide or Lyons. Climate makes the biggest difference to what people wear. Slip-on shoes, white socks and flat-arse jeans are as common in Paris as in Kilburn.

In the countryside and smaller towns, the differences become more marked. There, people still dress as their grandparents did. Often, they are wearing the same garments as their grandparents, literally. At least they were made to last, even if that was obviously the only thing the makers had in mind.

There are few more pathetic sights than the rural French youth dressed up like a time warp from the English provinces in the mid-nineteen-seventies, heading for their nearest groovy bar to sip flat, weak beer and listen to Johnny Hallyday hits on the Juke Box. But they *feel* chic because they are French and the French, they feel, are chic.

If you decide to buy clothes, or anything else, in France you may find it harder than you think. The shops do not often open before 10 a.m., they shut for lunch by 1 p.m. and stay shut for two hours. In more rural areas, they often forget to re-open at all. Outside the cities, people hold little thanksgiving services just because they actually found somewhere open, but then they are a devoutly Catholic nation.

As in any situation where the French are providing a service to the public, it will be surly, grudging, mean and bad. So if you are feeling homesick in France, just go into a shop. Even the language barrier seems lower when the most you'll ever hear from people is a bad-tempered grunt.

A word of warning about trying to speak French in places like shops. If an assistant speaks a little English, as they tend to in places like Calais and Dunkirk, they go all huffy if you try to talk to them in French. Often, they pretend not to understand you.

The best rule of conduct if you're with someone who also speaks English is, therefore, as follows. Talk in God's Own Language to each other. If the assistant then uses English with you, go along with them. If they annoy you, start speaking in poor French. They will pretend they cannot follow you. Then use some of the following insults, being careful with the pronunciation. When they start screaming back at you in French, pretend *you* don't understand *them.*

I'm not interrupting, am I?

J'espère que je ne vous interrompe pas.

<Jays-spare ka june voo-sun-tear-romp pah>

A kilo of Gouda, please.

Un kilo de Gouda, s'il vous plaît.

<Unk key-low dug gouda, seal voo play>

And two hundred and fifty grams of Stilton.

Et deux cent cinquante grammes de Stilton.

<Aid-does-sont sank-aunt gram dust Stilton>

I'm looking for a good quality wine, something Californian, perhaps.

Je cherche un vin de bonne qualité, quelque-chose de Californien, peut-être.

<Josh-share-shun van dub-on ka-lea-tay, kelk-ash-shows duck-caliph-fawn-ian, put-ate-Ra>

No? Chilean, then?

Non? Donc, Chilean?

<Gnaw? Donk, chill-ian>

Are these mushrooms safe?

Les champignons, sont-ils à manger sans risque?

<Lay champ-in-yon saunt-eel a morn-jay son risk>

Not as good as English clothes, are they?

Ils ne sont pas aussi chic que les vêtements anglais, n'est-ce pas?

<Eel song pa's so-sea sheeck cool lay vet-morn sawn-glay, nest pa>

I'm sorry, I don't understand you.

Je m'excuse, mais je vous comprends pas.

<Jew mex-kews, may jew voo comp-prawn pa>

Off to a fancy dress party, then?

Vous allez au bal costumé, quoi?

<Voo-sah-lay oh bawl cause-to-may, kwa>

Nice suit. I had one like that in the seventies.

Joli complet. J'en avais un de pareil dans les années soixante-dix.

<Jolly com-play. John'ave-eh under par-ay dawn lay san-nay swa-sont-deece>

What a lovely dress! Did you make it yourself?

Quelle jolie robe! L'avez vous faites vous même?

<Kel jolly rob! Lav-eh voo fate voo maim>

What a witty tie!

Quelle cravate plein d'esprit.

<Kel kra-vat plain day-spree>

6. Describing Physical Appearance

General De Gaulle was born to symbolise France. His name, of course, was uncanny, as improbable as a British politician being called Brittan. But his appearance marked him out to perhaps a greater degree. He was very tall, which is unusual in France, but otherwise he looked like a composite of French facial characteristics.

In his youth, he had a weak chin, huge nose and watery little eyes, widely spaced to give almost 360° vision (a useful survival adaptation). His long thin neck weaved like a plant stalk inside the oversized circle of his collar, large protruding Adam's apple sliding into and out of sight as he spoke. When they looked at him, every Frenchman could see a part of their own reflection; every French woman, a favourite uncle or brother. This was, of course, a major element in his popularity.

Then, like many wartime leaders, his star waned and he lost office. Age brought its consolations; he, naturally, became fatter. There was a new wave of public sympathy for him and he was re-elected. Obesity has always been popular in a nation of gourmands like the French. Buttock enlargement, giving that prized "inflated by footpump" look, has become a fashionable cosmetic operation, enhancing the already famous pear shaped profile of French women.

French women are also well-known for the pride they take in their hair, carefully plaiting and highlighting it in places where their sisters from other countries normally shave.

Obviously, the French do not all look like these stereotypes. After all, this is the country which produces women like Brigitte Bardot, and men like... ah, you know, ex-politician or something. English name. Jack Lang. And, apparently, there was another good looking Frenchman around the turn of the century. But, on the whole, they are not a nation blessed with superficial beauty. Let's rub their oversized noses in it, shall we?

Have you ever done any modelling?

Etiez-vous jamais mannequine?

<Ate-tea-eh voo jammy man-ache-keen>

Good God, you're ugly.

Bon Dieu, vous etes laid.

<Born dew, voos eight laid>

I expect some people find French looks quite attractive.

Je crois que quelque persons trouvent le mien français assez beau.

<Jack-Ra cuck-elk-cap-person troove lamb me-yen france-say a-say bow>

Has anyone ever saddled you, by mistake?

Personne vous a jamais sellé par erreur?

<Person voo-sah jammy sell-ape par error>

Why are the French so ugly? Bad diet, no doubt.

Pourquoi les français sont-ils si laids? Une régime mauvaise, sans doute.

<Poor-kwa lay france-say sawn-teal seal aid? Oon ray-gym mauve-eh, sawn-doot>

The poor girl looks really *French*.

La pauvre fille paraît vraiment *française*

<Lap-pour-vruh fee par-eh vray-mont france-says>

With good visibilty, can you see the far end of your nose?

Avec une bonne visibilité, vous le voyez le but de votre nez?

<Ah-veck youn bon visa-billy-tay, voo-love-why-yale a-boot dove vot nay>

Would you like some mud to roll in, or something.

Voudriez-vous de la boue pour y rouler?

<Voo-dree-eh-voo dull-lab-boo pour E rule>

Cosmetic surgery is quite affordable nowadays.

La chirurgie cosmétique est très abordable de nos jours.

<Lash-sheer-urge-she cosmet-E.K. trays abord-dabble dunno jaw>

7. Unwelcome Romantic Encounters

Are there such things? Depends, normally, on how much you've had to drink and which gender you are. Women seem to find attempted pick-ups unwelcome more often than men. There are, however, exceptions.

If a man is approached in Paris, especially but not exclusively in the area of the Bois de Boulogne, he would do well to remember that many of the most attractive women there are not, in fact, women. Most men would notice something was wrong as the evening wore on, but you might not want to get into such a position, as it were, in the first place.

Of course, if you do, check out the Bois de Boulogne. Seek out someone of Brazilian appearance. Try some subtle question like 'Excuse me, Miss, have you ever been a man?' **('Excusez-moi, Mademoiselle, étiez-vous jamais un homme?'** <Ex-ewes-eh-mwa, Mah-mwa-zell, ate-tea-ay voo jammy zan om?>) A reply of **'Oui'** (<Wee>) would mean 'Yes'. I'm not sure what, in this instance, the French for 'No' would be.

For women, the risks are higher. The French are second only to the Italians in the mistaken self-image stakes. At any moment, you could be approached by someone sounding like Charles Aznavour on Mogadon, muttering things like **'Ma Cherie',** and **'Oh! Vous êtes si belle!',** while drops of sweat fall from his chin onto his purple kipper tie.

Obviously, some of the pithier responses possible in these situations can be gleaned from the Quick-Reference Insult Guide at the back of this book. Some more sentence-like options follow.

Incidentally, watch out for the verb **'baiser'** (<bay-zay>). According to most dictionaries, this means 'to kiss'. In street use, it doesn't. It means 'to fuck'. Thus, **'Je voudrais vous baiser'** (<Shuh voo-dray voo bay-zay>, 'I would like to "baiser" you') may not be as innocent as it seems.

I've just had some bad news from the clinic. I'd prefer to be alone right now. Do you mind?

Excusez-moi, mais j'aimerais être toute seule en ce moment. Je viens de recevoire des mauvaises nouvelles de la clinique.

<Ex-ews-say-mwa, may shay-may-ray ate-ruh toot surl on same mow-maw. Shove vee-end duh russ-sah-vwa day mo-vays noo-Well duh lah clean-nick>

Tell me, have you let Jesus into your life yet?

Dites-moi, avez vous déjà accepté Jesu dans votre vie?

<Deet-mwa, ah-Way voo day-jah ux-ep-tay Yea-sue don vot-trav-vee)

Good Lord! My Doctor friend, Denise, would like to meet *you*. She specialises in tropical diseases.

Bon Dieu! Denise, mon amie médécin, aimerais beaucoup vous rencontrer. Elle fait la spécialité des maladies tropicales.

<Born dew! Denise, mon ah-me med-san, ay-may-ray bow-coup voo ron-con-tray. El fay la spay-see-al-lit-tay day mull-adee tro-pee-cal>

I'm sorry, I can't talk to you right now. My boyfriend is due back any minute from his 'controlling violent jealousy' group therapy meeting.

Je m'excuse, je ne peux pas vous parler là. Mon fiancé rentre d'un moment à l'autre d'une cours pour le contrôl de la jalousie violente.

<Jew mex-kews, John puh pah voo par-lay lah. Mon fee-an-say ron-tray dawn mow-maw a law-truh doon cor poor lah con-troll duh lash-shall-loo-sea vee-oh-launt>

It's amazing, you look so much like my Grandfather!

C'est incroyable, vous resemblez tout à fait mon grand-père.

<Say ankh-roy-ah-bluh, voo russ-sawm-blay toot a-fay mong gron-pear>

Would you like to use this napkin? There's some dribble on your chin.

Voulez-vous cette serviette? Y'a de la bavure sur votre menton.

<Voo-lay-voo set sir-viet? Yah duh lah bav-you're sir vot mon-toh>

Do I fancy a good time? Yes. As soon as you've gone, I'm going to have one.

J'aimerais un bon temps? Oui. Ça viendra lorsque vous seriez parti.

<Jay-moray sun bon tom? Wee. Sah vee-on-dra laws-curve-ooze savvy party, john or ray a-vwah>

Part 3
Dealing With The French Authorities

1. Clearing Customs

French customs, or **'Douane',** have the strange habit of stopping people on their way out of the country. You'd have thought that, if the travellers are carrying anything that is banned or illegal in France, they'd be glad to see the back of it. But no.

A few simple rules will help smooth your passage through a customs spot check. For example, if asked whether you packed your suitcases yourself, don't reply 'No, a nice Algerian called Ahmed did it for me.'

If you are claiming that the fifty-thousand

Marlboro they found under a travel rug in the boot of your car are for personal consumption, it's best to have at least two cigarettes on the go at all times. This is, in fact, quite normal in France anyway. French smokers fall into two categories: all the men in the country, and all the women in the country. Health faddism hasn't yet taken the country by storm. It will be some years before you see a French President jogging with his bodyguards.

Anyone carrying more than ten cases of beer would be well advised to keep a dozen cheap cigars in their pocket. If stopped by the customs, offer them around immediately. Your claim that it is your niece's third wedding that month will be more likely to be believed. 'This time it's for keeps,' you should explain (**'Cet fois, c'est pour toujours',** <Set fwah say pour too-sure>). They won't stop you leaving with it if they are sceptical, but the malicious bastards will 'phone their British counterparts, who will confiscate it. And how will you explain that to your misty-eyed niece?

Of course, if you are caught with 20,000

ecstasy tablets, you're going to find it difficult to talk your way out of the situation. Being a peasant nation, horny-handed sons of the soil, they are unlikely to accept that you only use them to get closer to God. Maybe you should try to blame Ahmed, who helped with your suitcases. Whatever you say, I expect you are likely to want to refer to the next three chapters. We do try to provide a comprehensive service here.

No, a nice Algerian called Ahmed did it for me.*

Non, Ahmed, un gentil Algérien l'a fait pour moi.

<Gnaw, Ach-med, uh john-tea Al-share-ree-ah lah fay pour mwa>

I'm a bit pressed for time. Could you pull your finger out?

Je suis un peu pressé. Vous pouvez vous grouiller?

<Jus'-wee uh puh press-say. Voo poo-vay voo grew-yee-eh>

*Don't say I didn't warn you.

What a nice dog. Would it like an aniseed drop?

Quel chien sympa. Aimerait-il un bonbon à l'anis?

<Kell shyeah sam-pah. Aim-er-ray-teal uh boh-boh Al a-knee>

I don't think the boot opens. I never use it, you see.

Je crois que le coffre ne s'ouvert pas. Je ne le utilise jamais, voyez.

<Jack-rah cull-luck-cough nurse who've pa. June-nuh-luh you-till-ease jammy, why-eh>

It's my niece's wedding on Saturday.
She's a heavy smoker.

C'est le mariage de ma nièce samedi prochain.
Elle fume beaucoup.

<Say lah marry-arge duh mah knee-yes sam-dee prosh-shane. Ell foom bow-coo>

I'm as surprised as you are. What do you think it could be? Icing sugar?

J'en suis aussi surpris que vous. Qu'est ce que vous pensez ça pourrait être? Du sucre glace?

<John swee-sew-see sir-pree kuh voo. Kes-kuh voo pawn-say sah poo-rate ate-ruh? Doo sue-kray glass>

I warn you, I've got friends in high places. My wife's maiden name is Chirac.

Je vous previens, j'ai des amis très bien placés. Le nom de jeune fille de ma femme c'est Chirac.

<Juh voo prove-yen, jay Des ah-me tray b'yen plass-say. Luh noh duh john feed ma famm say She-rack>

2. Dealing With Police

Best, in some ways, to be polite. Though not as trigger-happy as the Belgians, who ask you to stop by firing three rounds into your car radiator, these hombres are armed. And they're generally dying to get a chance to use their weapons, not having done so since the last time they opened fire. It's some sort of macho overcompensation and, since they are of course French, we shouldn't judge them too harshly. They've a lot to overcompensate for.

Strictly, the Police operate in the towns and the **Gendarmes,** who are not Police, police the countryside. You can tell the **Gendarmes** from their semi-military uniforms and their silly saucepan hats. They answer to the Ministry of Defense, or **Ministère de la Défense,** as we fluent French speakers call it.

If you are stopped by either the Police or the Gendarmes, show them some papers. Any papers, so long as they look fairly official. A library card would be better than nothing. Like most illiterate people, they are easily impressed by the written word and tend to assume that your documents must be authorisation for whatever it is you happen to be doing.

There's another group, the CRS (**compagnies républicaines de sécurité,** or state security police), who deal with riots and demonstrations. They are probably the most hated people in France. You should definitely be courteous if you meet these boys, unless you want to experience some of the best in Gallic dental adjustment.

The following phrases are actually very commonly used by the French in reference to their police, though not necessarily to their face. The tradition of rioting is deeply entrenched in France. Everyone does it, from students to farmers.

A lot of abuse is actually quite specific to the police. There is a type of French slang which involves switching the first and last halves of a word. Thus, **'pourri'** (<pooh-ree>), or 'rotten', becomes **'ripoux'** (<ree-pooh>). But **'un ripoux'** is a bent copper. The usual slang term for a cop is **'un flic'** <uh fleeck>.

There is, though I'm reluctant to admit it, an excellent film called **'Le Ripoux',** a comedy which charts the fall from grace of an idealistic young detective who is transferred from a rural department to work with **'un ripoux'.** Let's pass hurriedly on to the insults.

Flush the cops down the toilet
Aux chiottes les flics.*
<Oh shee-ot lay fleeck>

Filthy cops
Sale flics*
<Sull fleeck>

* frequently shouted from a distance, or from barricades

Good morning/afternoon/evening officer. What a pleasure to see you.
Bonjour/bonsoir monsieur l'agent. Quel plaisir de vous voir.
<Bore-sure/bore-swa muss-your lah-john. Kell play-seer duh voo vwah>

Shouting? Not me. I have enough trouble speaking French, let alone shouting, ha ha ha.
Gueuler? Moi pas. Je peux à peine parler le français, moins encore gueuler, ha, ha, ha.
<Girl-lay? Mwa pah. Juh puh ah pain pa-lay luh frawn-say, mwa on-core girl-lay, ha, ha, ha>

Here are my papers. No, no - this way up.
Voici mes papiers. Non, non - vous les avez à l'envers.
<Vwa-see may pap-pea-yeah. Gnaw, gnaw - voo lace savvy Al on-vair>

That cash in my passport? I'd forgotten it was there. Why don't you hang on to it?

L'argent dans mon passport? Je l'avais tout à fait oublié. Pourquoi ne le gardez-vous pas?

<Lah-john don moh pass-poor. Jill lavvy toot ah fate ooh-belay. Pork-wah null leg-guard-day voo pa>

I warn you, I've got friends in high places. My wife's maiden name is Chirac.

Je vous previens, j'ai des amis très bien placés. Le nom de jeune fille de ma femme c'est Chirac.

<Juh voo prove-yen, jay Des ah-me tray b'yen plass-say. Luh noh duh john feed ma famm say She-rack>

3. The French Judicial System

France is the country of **'droit de l'homme',** which translates literally as 'human rights', but has overtones of law and order, **'droit'** being a French expression for law, or legal rights. The French are very proud of their legal system and, rather like their armed forces, it is an institution for which most of them feel deep reverence. Obviously, if they hear a foreigner criticise it, they become very twitchy.

Parallels with their armed forces continue: their legal system is crap. In comparison, Southern Italy looks noble and idealistic. The main effect of the French system today is to keep the number of North Africans on the streets down to what Jean Marie le Pen would consider to be a manageable level.

To give a fundamental example, their equivalent of proving someone's guilt 'beyond reasonable doubt' is the principle of **'intime conviction'** (inner certainty). The court must have an inner certainty that a defendant is guilty before convicting them, regardless of the weight of evidence. In practice, if the judges reckon the accused is guilty, they will convict on the grounds that they have an **'intime conviction'** of the person's guilt, even if there is little or no evidence in the case.

Under their inquisitorial system, the case against an accused is investigated by a judge, the **'juge d'instruction'.** In theory, this person is an impartial examiner of the case who should be as concerned for the benefit of the defendant as for the interests of the prosecutor. In practice they are often young and anxious to make a name for themselves, which is not done by letting people go. Thus, they act as a second prosecutor. They have no part in the sentencing of the convicted person which means, as you might have guessed if you are getting the hang of this, that they sentence them by way of informal recommendation.

The equivalent of legal aid pays a defence lawyer 700FFrs, or about £90, for the whole case. Obviously, they can only just afford to turn up during the trial for this sort of money. They certainly can't be expected to do anything. If they do, they are rare, idealistic and basically working for free. This all discriminates against the poor, immigrants, the underprivileged ... all those who should benefit from **'droits de l'homme'.**

Your legal system is copied the world over, from Burkina Faso to Mali.

Votre système judiciaire est copié partout dans le monde, depuis Burkina Faso jusqu'au Mali.

<Vott see-stem jew-dee-sea-air ay cop-pea-yea par-two don luh mond, dup-wee Burr-keen-ah Far-so jusk-oh Ma-lee>

This has all been a terrible misunderstanding. But I can explain everything.

Il y'a eu un affreux malentendu. Mais je peux tout expliquer.

<Eel-yah ooh oon aff-ruse mal-on-ton-due. May juh puh toot ex-plea-kay>

You have a wonderful tradition of human rights. What a shame you ignore it.

Vous avez un tradition des droits de l'homme magnifique. C'est dommage que vous l'ignorez.

<Voo savvy uh trah-dees-your day drah duh lom mag-niff-eek. Say dom-marge kuh voo lag-gnaw-ray>

I left the car unlocked in Calais, I suppose someone could have planted it then.

A Calais je n'ai pas bouclé la voiture, je suppose que quelqu'un aurrait pu y mettre quelque chose.

<Ah Kall-lay juh nay pah boo-clay lah what-you're, juh soup-pose kuh kell-kun or-ray poo ee met-rah kelk-shows>

I met a man in a pub.

J'ai rencontré un type dans un bar.

<Jay ron-con-tray uh teep don's an bar>

I've got a great idea. You let me go, and I'll lead you to them.

J'ai une bonne idée. Vous me laissez aller, et je vous les trouve.

<Jay you'n bonny-day. Voo muh lay-say allay, eh juh voo lay troove>

No, honestly. Trust me.

Non, vraiment. Faut me faire confiance.

<Gnaw, frame-mont. Fo muh fair con-fee-yonce>

I warn you, I've got friends in high places. My wife's maiden name is Chirac.

Je vous previens, j'ai des amis très bien placés. Le nom de jeune fille de ma femme c'est Chirac.

<Juh voo prove-yen, jay Des ah-me tray b'yen plass-say. Luh noh duh john feed ma famm say She-rack>

4. French Prisons

Oh dear. Maybe you have made rather too much use of this book. That, or the **juge d'instruction** did not believe your explanation about the ecstasy the customs found in your car. Before you start blaming us, remember this is all meant to be read out of purely academic interest and not used in real life. Did we forget to make that clear? How careless.

At least you'll now have plenty of time to work on your French. Think of it as a free immersion course in the language. The days of Papillon are long gone. You won't be sent to Devil's Island.

The French are readying that for their nuclear testing. After all, it's only a matter of time before they are sent packing from the Pacific. No, you'll be in the lap of luxury; at least, that's what the newspapers say. 'Continental Prisoners Don't Want To Go Home', is a regular space-filler for certain members of the British fourth estate.

In reality, you probably won't like being in prison. Few people do. Although Britain leads the European incarceration stakes, with more people per capita in jail than any other European Union member, France is trying desperately to catch up. They've never liked being one-upped by the Brits. So you'll find it very crowded. But there may be some compensations.

You'll meet a lot of fellow countrymen there. In the main, they are banged up for narcotics offences. France does, after all, lie between both Spain and Holland, and the shortest route across the English Channel. If you are a drug smuggler, this will be of great professional benefit. Most gaols there are like international merchant-of-death conferences. You'll be able to plan lots of new capers and make all sorts of invaluable contacts.

If you're a trafficker, with serious money, rather than a poor courier, you'll also be able to, in effect, buy yourself out under their inspired system of customs fines, so it won't go on so long it gets too boring.

And who says prison doesn't work?

However, you are going to need a few simple phrases to assist with your day to day functioning. Being abusive in gaol can have its downside. This is called 'the block' in English, the **'mitard'** <meter> in French. It's up to you. Some of the following phrases are designed for use with the guards, or **'surveillants'** <survey-onts>, others for your fellow inmates. If you want to switch them around, on your own head be it.

Certainly, Mr Warder.

Bien sûr, Monsieur le Surveillant.

<B-yen sir, maws-yuh luh serve-ay-ont>

Are you looking for a slap, shitface?

Tu veux une baffe, connard?

<Too vuh oon baff, con-are>

It's all been a misunderstanding. My lawyer will have me out of here in a week.

Il y'a eu un malentendu. Mon avocat va me tirer d'ici en moins d'une semaine.

<Eel-yah ooh an mal-on-ton-due. More nav-oh-car muh tear-ray D.C. on mwa dune suh-main>

Which one of you bastards stole my trousers?

Lequel de vous salauds m'a piqué mes pantalons?

<Look-ell duh voo sallow mah pea-kay may pant-tallow>

No, you don't understand. I'm innocent. Haven't you got a nicer room for me?

Non, vous ne comprenez pas. Je suis innocent. Vous n'avez pas une chambre plus sympa pour moi?

<Gnaw, voon com-prawn-nay pah. Juh swees ann-no-song. Voo navvy pah soon shawm-burr plews sam-pah pour mwa>

I'm not very artistic. Get someone else to tattoo your forehead for you.

Je ne suis pas très artistique. Trouve quelqu'un d'autre pour te tatouer le front.

<John swee pah tray sah-tease-teak. Troove kell-kun dort porter tattoo-ay luh frong>

I warn you, I've got friends in high places. My wife's maiden name is Chirac.

Je vous previens, j'ai des amis très bien placés. Le nom de jeune fille de ma femme c'est Chirac.

<Juh voo prove-yen, jay Des ah-me tray b'yen plass-say. Luh noh duh john feed ma famm say She-rack>

Part 4
Conversation Topics

1. French Culture

The French are immensely proud of their culture. It is, therefore, very easy to make them feel offended either about specific aspects of it, as will be covered in following chapters, or in general.

They are particularly sensitive about the fact that rather than absorb and celebrate all things French, which would seem to them to be the obvious thing to do, the world is in fact taking on English speaking culture at breakneck speed. As we all know, this is a natural development, but try telling that to anyone of a Gallic persuasion.

They are deeply proud of their language, and someone who speaks perhaps two languages, their own and, normally, English, will have no hesitation in telling you that French is the most beautiful, expressive and richest tongue in the whole world. They've never even heard someone speak, say, Farsi, but they can tell you French is better.

Well, O.K., they'll tell you, English is becoming the international language of business. It is, in its way, quite functional. But you couldn't write great literature in it.

Oddly, the opposite is more true. I'm told that French has been kept 'pure' to the extent where it lacks the polylingual synonyms available in English. If I knew what that meant, I might be able to comment. In any event, it seems Samuel Beckett wrote in French because he liked the unambiguous nature of the language. It's a relief to be able to explain that one, I can tell you.

In the absence of a complex language, they fall back on quantity and gloom. A sixteen volume epic saga following four generations of a fictitious family of congenitally suicidal weavers from Flanders would be almost guaranteed to win the **Prix Goncourt,** a French literary equivalent of the Booker prize, but without the money or, to anyone but the French, prestige.

Gloom and difficulty are, of course, meat and drink to French thinkers. The word **'intellectuel'** is very difficult to translate. It is not a term of abuse, like the English word 'intellectual', but refers to a class of person which exists only in France. Those who make a fetish out of thought.

British Prime Ministers boast that they never went to school. If a Rhodes Scholar becomes U.S. President, he has to immediately start talking about 'folks' and 'grits'. In Australia, political advancement makes accomplished graduates start swearing like itinerant sheep shearers. But in France, the bookshelves teeter under the weight of fatuous political theories written by every would-be politician, which are presented as complete answers to every problem the world has ever faced, and then forgotten ten minutes later. This is the work of would-be **'intellectuels'**.

When at rest, real ones pose like Rodin sculptures, chin on fist. In movement, the tosses of the head and the rapid hand movements give them away. If you have the misfortune to speak to one, he or she will expect you to write down their every word and preserve it for a grateful posterity. Intelectuels are everywhere there is a bookshop or a school, but most particularly they are to be found in Paris.

Traditionally, the fashionable young turks have been left-wing, able to range free in their imaginations because there has never been the slightest possibility that any of their ideas will be attempted. On the right, the select few in **L'Academie française** have tried to act as brakemen on French evolution. They have, in their own eyes, sole custody of the French language, although they allow the rest of the population visiting rights.

But all of them are pompous, self-important, verbose, unnecessarily complicated and boring - mind-numbingly, desperately dull. They hide simple, and often fatuous, ideas behind deliberate and unnecessary obscurantism. For example, Jacques Derrida is generally credited as having helped found the most important school of literary criticism in recent decades, Deconstruction. Here, he explains in a letter to a Japanese friend what this theory is and is not.

> 'What Deconstruction is not?
> Everything, of course!
> What Deconstruction is?
> Nothing, of course!"

Of course I'm learning French. It's the seventh most important language in the world.

Bien sûr que j'apprends le français. C'est la septième en importance des langues de monde.

<Be-yen sewer, kuh jap-prawn luh fron-say. Say lah sap-tea-aim awe amp-or-tawnce day long duh mond>

I love French - such a simple language.

J'aime le français - une langue tellement simple.

<Jay-muh luff-fron-say - oon long tell-lamont sam-pluh>

Of course, it's hard to motivate yourself when you already speak English.

Bien sûr, quand on parle l'anglais il est difficile de se motiver.

<Be-yen sewer, con-on par-lay-yon-glay eel aid diff-is-seal does some-motive-eh>

Did you know, English already includes most French words?

Savez-vous que le vocabulaire anglais comprends la plus parte des mots français?

<Savvy voo colour vocab-you'll-air yon-glay comp-prawn lap-loo part day mauve fron-say>

And English has four times as many words in its vocabulary as French.

Et l'anglais a quatre fois plus de mots dans son vocabulaire que le française.

<Ale-long-lay a cat fwap-loo day-mow don son vocab-you-lair colour france-say>

Maybe you could help. Last night we were trying to think of a famous living French writer.

Peut-être vous pourriez m'aider? Hier soir, nous n'arrivons pas a nous rappeller d'un seul écrivain de marque français vivant.

<Put-ate-rave-voo poo-ree-eh may-day? Ee-air swan noon a-reeve-on pa's a new wrap-pell-eh done sir'll eck-reeve-van dumb mark france-say veeve-on>

I find the *German* existentialists so much more interesting, don't you?

Je trouve les existentialists allemands tellement plus interessent, vous pas?

<Jut roof lays exist-awn-seal-list al-morn tell-lamont plew santa-rest-aunt, voo pa>

2. Entertainment

•••••••••••••••••••••••••••••••••••••

French T.V. is brilliant if you like crappy films, back-to-back dubbed re-runs of Miami Vice and variety shows which last for hours and are like 'Blankety Blank' without the wit. Or, indeed, the celebrities, prizes, subtlety or intellectual stimulation. Think of a lobotomised version of 'The Generation Game' without any competitions or guests and you have **'Coucou, C'est Nous',** which is dished up for two hours in the early evening by **TF1,** then reprised after the ten o'clock watershed for another two hours and guess what? It's just as bland and numbingly dull as it was before!

There are two French Film Stars, Gerard Depardieu and Jean-Paul Belmondo. All the rest are Belgian or, like Catherine Deneuve, act in English language films whenever possible.

Belmondo appears in normally low budget, though sometimes well financed, action films. Depardieu, by contrast, has made mainly low budget action films, though sometimes well financed cinema 'classics'. Predictably, he has been learning English.

'Action', however, normally has a different meaning in French. As often as not, it means watching Depardieu driving a couple of teenage thugs around in a battered, ten-year-old Citroen (as if there's any other kind in France), throwing up a lot of dust and engaging in occasional inarticulate exchanges with each other and the few people they meet. The overall effect is rather like a fast car chase without the 'fast' or the 'chase'.

There will always be some gunfire, perhaps at the beginning, definitely at the end. If there's a lot of it, or it sounds like automatic weapons, and if you're watching it on T.V., you probably dozed off during the Depardieu film and have been woken by the climax of the Belmondo one which followed it.

This means you missed the bit where Depardieu and his pals screwed an Older Woman in a roadside adventure AND the bit where Belmondo's ravishing half-Japanese wife was strip-searched by the French Intelligence services pretending to be the police, while he rogered the head cop's wife on a narrow ledge fourteen floors up the side of an apartment building, before returning home to 'console' his wife. So, you blew it, figuratively speaking.

The comedy films are very funny, if you are amused by late-middle-aged transvestites with falsetto voices and pretensions to respectability, or by the sight of a guide dog leading its master under a steam roller.

Then there are the Art films. Only possible under a 'quota' system, I'm afraid. Twenty minutes of black and white footage showing a man wearing the top half of a Cossack uniform with a tutu, tights and wellies, carrying a double-bass case across a windswept winter field to a corrugated tin hut in the middle of a vast emptiness where he spins a plate on a stick until the closing seconds, when he is joined by a shaven headed, corpse like girl in a transparent graveyard shift, who leads a bespectacled llama, towing an upright piano in a trailer, into the frame.

Brilliant, no doubt, to those who like that sort of stuff.

The biggest French Rock Star of all time is a Belgian dwarf called Johnny Hallyday. A typical stadium concert will include him posing by a Harley Davidson motorcycle, wearing a late-period-Elvis spandex jumpsuit with ten inch high sequinned collars, singing 'Johnny B. Goode' in French, while his band plays 'Roll Over Beethoven'.

Johnny Hallyday is, you will have gathered, the best French pop music has to offer. He is like Elvis, Cliff Richards and the Beatles all rolled into one - a sort of musical version of a road accident. Part of his continuing appeal is that there have never been any other French pop stars. This is a country in which a busker playing a sugary medley of Beatles hits can hold the number one spot in the singles charts for ten consecutive weeks.

Their biggest claim to popular musical fame lies in the fact that the song 'My Way' was originally written in French, when it was called **'Comme Habitude'** <comm a-bit-you'd-uh>. Of course, this song only achieved its success after it was translated into English.

Mind you, France's geographical situation means it also imports some of the best in German, Romanian and Italian rock. **'Megamix',** a weekly music programme on the cable channel **'Arte'**, has even been known to bring Mongolian throat singing to its audience. After hourly repeats of **'Si tu es là, je serais là'** (If you are there, I will be there), Johnny Hallyday's 1993/4 blockbuster, filmed live at the Parc des Princes, on **M6** (the crappiest channel on French T.V.), you start to notice a strange foot-tapping quality in those Mongolian vibes.

You'll also hear quite a lot of excellent

North African music, recorded in the few years available to Algerian musicians between attaining adulthood and being assassinated by the **FIS** (Islamic Salvation Front).

Of course, this music isn't French.

In all French popular culture, there is an obsession with very young, pre-pubescent-looking girls, or **'gamines',** <gamm-een>. You will see them presenting or appearing on television programmes, starring in films ('Nikita', for example) or making pop records (Vanessa Paradise). The key to understanding this was provided by Jane Birkin in a film she made years ago with Serge Gainsbourg, her lover.

A **gamine** herself at the time, Birkin is sodomised by a lorry driver, screaming 'I am your boy' as it happens. The French are, of course, almost without exception closet homosexuals who cover it up by talking loudly about being great lovers, while at the same time elevating to stardom boyish girls whose sole claim to fame is that they are, well, boyish. Need I say more?

Eat your heart out, Edith Cresson.

'Interesting T.V. last night. I think it was a theme evening for people with learning difficulties.'

Une télé interessent hier soir. Ca a du être une soirée de programmes pour les arriérés.

<Oon tell-lay ant-err-rest-aunt tea-yeah swah. Sah ah dew ate-rahoon swah-radar prog-rom pour lays 'arry-air-ray>

'I was watching TF1 yesterday - or was it France 3? They all blend into one.'

Hier j'ai regardé TF1 - ou peut être France 3? Ils sont si semblables.

<Ee-yeah jay regard-day tay-eff-uh - ooh put-ate-rough france twa. Eel song see somme-blahb>

British television is so much better, don't you think?

Je trouve la télé britannique beaucoup mieux, vous pas?

<Jut-roof lat-tel-lay britain-eek boo-coomb me-yer, voo-pa>

Tell me, are there any good French films?

Dites moi, y'a-t-il de bons films français?

<Deet-mwa, yat-eel duh bon feelm frawn-say>

No, we don't dub them into English. There's no point. Nobody would watch them.

Non, on ne fait pas le doublage à l'anglais. Ce n'est pas la peine. Personne ne les regarderait pas.

<Gnaw, on nuff-ape parlour doob-large al long-lay. Sir nay pa lap pain. Person nuh lay regard-er-ape pa>

I like French films. Makes me realise how good British ones are.

J'aime les films français, moi. Ils me font comprendre que les fims britanniques sont si bons.

<Jay malay film france-say. Eel muff-font comp-prawn-druh cool-lay film britain-eek song see bon>

There are some excellent French actors. Of course, they all learn English and go to Hollywood.

Il y a des comediêns français excellents. Bien sûr, ils apprennent tous l'anglais et vont à Hollywood.

<Eel-yard-day comm-heed-yen france-say excell-lawnt. Be-yen sewer eel sap-prawn toose lawn-glay avon ta olly-wood>

3. Politics

President De Gaulle once asked 'How can anyone hope to rule a country that makes five hundred different cheeses?' Of course, he is most famous for hoping to rule France. Perhaps he was getting confused.

This would have been understandable. The French are deeply proud of their revolution which, more than two centuries ago, removed the monarchy, dis-established the aristocracy and set up a republic with a fine constitution, which has ever since been completely ignored. But it's the thought that counts.

Perhaps because they enjoyed the first one so much, they have since set up a further four republics. And a couple of imperial regimes, a semi-constitutional monarchy and the odd military dictatorship. The present, fifth republic manages to combine many of the best features of all these systems.

A bewildering variety of political parties nominate candidates for elections to one Presidency, two chambers of Parliament, hundreds of town mayor offices and the European Parliament. It's hard to keep track of them all when parties spring up constantly, founded by strange dis-established aristocrats and Anglo-French businessmen, to take an absurd hypothetical example, but they are all basically of the right.

Mitterand was a good example. He was an International Socialist who lived in a Palace, revived medieval royal habits, such as granting pardons and remission to convicted prisoners, built vast monuments to France's Imperial Glory, continued with a colonial policy which stretched to the bombing of the Rainbow Warrior in New Zealand and operated an isolationist policy of trade protectionism.

Other characters include Jean Marie le Pen, a thirties-style fascist. It was a waste of time saving France from the Nazis, because they have now thrown up, as it were, the biggest Nazi Party in modern Europe.

Balladur is a Gaullist who had the benefit of looking almost exactly like one of the Bourbon Kings, the very chaps the revolution got rid of. This was a great advantage in the recent election for what boils down to a seven year tenure of the throne. Chirac, in contrast, is a Gaullist who does not look like a Bourbon.

Chirac is not exactly funny, although he has some interesting mannerisms, so we live in hope. He, like many French people was never terribly good at geography at school. They seem unable to grasp the fact that their country is bordered by the Mediterranean, the Atlantic and a few other European countries. Their problems with Algeria and in the Pacific stem from the peculiar delusion that they are entitled to station some Legionnaires and a few warships in a small group of islands, for example, whose inhabitants are unable to defend themselves, and then claim that a slice of Polynesia is, as a result, now geographically part of France.

There is a hidden agenda, remarked a French politician recently, behind Australia's vehement objections to the resumption of French nuclear testing in the Pacific. It is that Australia is claiming France is not a Pacific or Asian power. Such a claim would, of course, be absolutely true. France is a European power with atavistic colonialist delusions.

The concept of **'France outre mer',** overseas France, is fascinating. This dictates that a part of, say, South America is as French as Lyons, simply because it was once colonised by the French.

French politicians are helped in this sort of idiocy by a pompous and ineffective media. This reaches its nadir in television current affairs analysis. Journalists who interview famous people are just tickled pink to be there, and keen to have their gravity and intelligence confirmed by the approval of the VIP they are talking to. Sometimes, they seem barely able to hold back from rubbing their head affectionately, like a cat, against the ankle of their interviewee.

A second-rate colonial power, after Britain, Spain and Portugal, France is trying to compensate by refusing to let go long after everyone else has granted independence to every colony which wanted it, and even some which didn't.

However, they still cling to the delusion that theirs is the first and best modern liberal democracy in the free world. In reality, they are more like the Chinese, with whom there are strong parallels. Bad company to keep, but the present nuclear testing controversy admits no other comparisons.

One really ought to remind them of this.

It's about time France was absorbed by the United Kingdom.

Il est temps que la France soit incorporé dans le Royaume-Uni.

<Eel lay tonka laff france swat in-cor-pour-eh don luh roy-ohm you-knee>

Two hundred years after Louis the Sixteenth, you have discovered elective kingship. Bravo.

Deux cent ans après Louis seize, vous avez découvert la monarchie élective. Bravo.

<Does-song on a-pray Loo-ee says, voo savvy day-coo-ver lemon-arcy ay-lec-teef. Bravo>

But people get the government they deserve.

Mais les peuples reçcoivent la gouvernement qu'ils méritent.

<Male-lay purple russ-suave lag-goo-vern-a-mont keel may-reet>

You don't have a republic. It's a comic-opera monarchy.

Vous n'avez pas une république. C'est une monarchie opéra comique.

<Voo navvy pa sun ray-pub-leek. Say tune moan-arcy op-air-ra com-eek>

If your nuclear tests are so safe, do them in the Central Massive.

Si vos essaies nucleaires sont si peu dangéreuses, faîtes-les dans le Massif Central.

<See vose essay new-clay-air song see pud don-ger-ruse, fate lay don luh mass-seef sent-raal>

Chirac? Who's that?

Chirac? C'est qui?

<She-rack? Sake key >

ES DEUX COUILL
WATERLOO

4. Insulting the French Armed Services

•••••••••••••••••••••••••••••••••••

You will find this one of the most rewarding areas of abuse. The French are absurdly sensitive about their military. Anything less than unqualified praise will be scrutinised for veiled insults by almost every French citizen you meet.

This is particularly true when they talk to a Briton. In all the centuries of cross-channel warfare, they never won a single naval engagement. Of the thirty-odd land battles since the English got bored with the Hundred Years War and went home, France won just a couple. Their greatest military hero, Napoleon, was ultimately defeated at Waterloo by you-know-who.

The past century or so has seen a pompous and self-important high command watch in disbelief on three occasions as their country was overrun, first by the Prussians then, after unification, by the Germans. By the time of the next war they had just about managed to prepare for the last.

They now maintain a small professional army which, despite being armed to the teeth with personal nuclear weapons, still focuses mainly on beating up or murdering unarmed Greenpeace protestors. The majority of the armed forces are conscripts, young people without the slightest wish to be in uniform who are, as a consequence, a danger to themselves, even when training.

Although many people assume the existence of the E.U. makes a major land war unlikely in Western Europe, this vast standing army is ready at all times, presumably to deflect any potential invasion by their violent and warlike neighbours, the Belgians.

Despite this unimpressive history, many French people feel their armed forces can do no wrong. They have not advanced since the Dreyfus Affair, a century ago, when an unassuming Jewish officer was amateurishly framed with spying for Germany. Despite being clearly innocent, he was convicted and shipped to Devil's Island.

France was torn in half between those who could not conceive of the army ever being wrong about anything, and those who disagreed with kippering people because they are Jewish. Eventually, Dreyfus was released, but you will still find French people who swear he was guilty.

The country would be better off if they demilitarised completely and just hired mercenaries if trouble came along. They'd have a healthier society, and be better defended.

Incidentally, being almost a Latin nation, they call the Falklands the 'Malvinas', and popular sympathy lies with the Argentines. There is also much support for the IRA, despite the fact that they have two separatist movements impinging on them, in the Basque country and on Corsica, which they cannot see as being in any way analogous.

Then there's Algeria. This is what Ireland would be like today for the British if the Potato Famine and Partition had happened in the 1950s then, when a Catholic dominated party won an election in the South, there had been a British sponsored military coup.

When it comes to matters military, their brains froth.

I can understand you being proud of your army.
After all, winning isn't everything.

Je comprends que tu es fier de ton armée.
Après tous, gagner n'est pas la chose la plus importante.

<Jew con-prawn ka two a fee-air da ton arm-may.
Ap-ray two, gan-yay nay pa la show-sa lap-plew
sahn-pour-taunt>

Nice hats. Do they wear them for a bet, or something?

Beaux chapeaux. Est-ce qu'ils les portent pour un pari ou quoi?

<Bo shah-po. Esk eel lay port poor ung paree oo kwa>

The Foreign Legion is pretty good. Of course, the soldiers are not French.

Le Légion étrangeur, ce n'est pas mal. Bien sûr, les soldâts ne sont pas français.

<La lay-john ay-tronj-air neigh palm-al.. Bee-an sewer, lay solder nur song pa fron-say>

Oh yeah? The Argentines had a conscript army, just like you.

Vraiment? Les Argentines avaient une armée de conscrits, comme vous.

<Vray-maw? Lay sarjon-teen avay oon arm-may duh con-scree, com voo>

Don't talk to me about Malvinas, you pouffe, we made bloody sure it stays the Falklands.

Ne me parle pas des Malvinas, pédé, nous avons assuré qu'ils restent les Falklands.

<Nuh muh parl pah day Mal-veen-ah, pay-day, noose av-on ass-your-ray keel rest lay Folk-lawned>

Stick to blowing up Greenpeace boats. It's a lot easier than fighting a proper army.

Il faut vous tenir à exploser les bateaux de Greenpeace. C'est beaucoup plus facile qu'un combat contre une vraie armée.

<Eel fow voo tin-ear ah explose-say lay bat-oh duh Greenpeace. Say bow-coo plew fass-eel cun com-bah con-truh ung vray arm-may>

Don't talk to me like that, you little cunt. If the Brits hadn't bailed you out twice, you'd be wearing leather shorts today.

Ne me parle pas comme ça, p'tit con. Si les Rosbifs ne vous avaient pas tiré d'affaire deux fois, vous portierez actuellement les shorts de cuir.

<Nuh muh parl pah com sah, tea cong'. Sea lay Ros-bif nuh voo savvy pah tea-ray duff-air duh fwah, voo port-tea-air-ray act-you-ell-lamont lay shore duh queer>

No, I haven't forgotten Napoleon. I haven't forgotten Waterloo either.

Non, je n'ai pas oublié Napoleon. Je n'ai pas oublié Waterloo non plus.

<Gnaw, juh nay pah zoo-be-lay Nap-oh-lay-on. Juh nay pah zoo-be-lay Waterloo gnaw plew>

Quick-Reference Insult Guide

Fuck Off	Vas te faire foutre	**Vat Fair Foo-truh**
Fuck you	Je t'emmerde	**Juh-tom-mare-duh**
Out of the way	Tire toi de là	**Tear-twa-duh-la**
Piss Off	Fous le camp	**Fool-luck-comp**
Don't Bug Me	Fais pas chier	**Fay pa shay**
Shut Up	La Ferme	**Laff Firm**
Bullshit	Connerie	**Connery**
Good Lord	Bon Dieu	**Bond-dew**
Fuck me	Putain	**Poo-tah**
My Arse	Mon cul	**Monk-who**
That's Nothing	C'est rien	**Say ree-an**
What Crap	Je m'en torche	**Juh mon torsh**
	C'est de la merde	**Say duh lamb-mare-duh**
It's Fucked	C'est foutu	**Say foo-too**
Disgusting	Dégueuelasse	**day-goo-lass**
Rotten	Pourri	**Poo-ree**
Bloody	Sacré	**Sack-ray**
Fucking	Putain de ...	**Poo-tah duh...**
Shitty	...de Merde	**...duh mare-duh**